JiGGLE
WiGGLE
PRANCE
by Sally Noll

FOR TORY

The full-color art work,
gouache paintings, was
mechanically color-separated
and reproduced in
four colors.
The text typeface
is Avant Garde Bold.

Publisher, Greenwillow Books,
a division of William
Morrow & Company, Inc.,
105 Madison Avenue,
New York, N.Y. 10016.
Printed in Hong Kong by
South China Printing Co.
First Edition

10 9 8 7 6 5 4 3 2 1

Library of Congress
Cataloging-in-Publication Data

Noll, Sally.

Jiggle wiggle prance.

Summary: Includes illustrations
of animals acting out such rhyming
action words as "pull, flop, hop"
and "dance, prance."

1. English language—Rhyme
—Juvenile literature.
2. Vocabulary—Juvenile literature.
[1. English language—Rhyme.
2. Vocabulary]   I. Title.
PE1517.N6 1987   428.1   86-18322
ISBN 0-688-06760-3
ISBN 0-688-06761-1 (lib. bdg.)

WALK

ROCK   DROP

PUSH

PULL FLOP

HOP   SPIN

DANCE

JIGGLE WIGGLE

PRANCE

FOLLOW   **FLY**

SWING

HOBBLE

WOBBLE   FLING

JUMP

RUN   RACE

SKIP   **TRIP**

PACE

RIDE

DRIVE

ROLL

SKATE **STRIDE**

STROLL

CLIMB

SLIDE   **FALL**

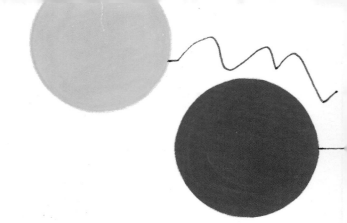

AND THAT'S ALL.